MW00783747

DEFINITE MAYBE PRODUCTIONS · MARK KRESS

in association with VICTORIA LANG & PIER PAOLO PICCOLI
and THE CENTURY CENTER FOR THE PERFORMING ARTS
present

Book by	Music by	Lyrics & Music by
NICHOLAS VAN HOOGSTRATEN	MARTIN SILVESTRI	JOEL HIGGINS

Based on the film produced by Republic Entertainment, Inc.
a subsidiary of Paramount Pictures, a Viacom company
and the novel by Roy Chanslor

starring

JUDY McLANE   ANN CRUMB   ROBERT EVAN

ED SALA   ROBB SAPP   DAVID SINKUS   JASON EDWARDS   GRANT NORMAN

and STEVE BLANCHARD as Johnny Guitar

Set Design	Lighting Design	Costume Design	Sound Design	Casting	Arrangements
VAN SANTVOORD	ED McCARTHY	KAYE VOYCE	LAURA GRACE BROWN	STEPHANIE KLAPPER	STEVE WIGHT

Music Director	Production Manager	Consulting Producer	Associate Producers	Press Representative	Marketing
JAMES MIRONCHIK	KAI BROTHERS	PAUL BLAKE	SARAH BROCKUS JEFFREY KENT	THE KARPEL GROUP	THE NANCY RICHARDS GROUP

Assistant Stage Manager	Production Stage Manager	Company Manager	General Manager	Associate Director	Choreography
PEGGY TAPHORN	MATTHEW LACEY	STEVEN DeLUCA	ROY GABAY	IAN BELTON	JANE LANIER

Directed by
JOEL HIGGINS

www.JohnnyGuitarTheMusical.com

Photos by Joan Marcus

ISBN 0-634-09503-X

7777 W. BLUEMOUND RD. P.O. BOX 13819 MILWAUKEE, WI 53213

In Australia Contact:
Hal Leonard Australia Pty. Ltd.
4 Lentara Court
Cheltenham, Victoria, 3192 Australia
Email: ausadmin@halleonard.com

Visit Hal Leonard Online at
www.halleonard.com

Ann Crumb, Judy McLane

Johnny

Judy McLane, Steve Blanchard, David Sinkus, Robert Evan, Robb Sapp

CONTENTS

JOHNNY GUITAR

Music by MARTIN SILVESTRI and JOEL HIGGINS
Lyrics by JOEL HIGGINS

LET IT SPIN

Music by MARTIN SILVESTRI and JOEL HIGGINS
Lyrics by JOEL HIGGINS

Light barroom Blues

VIENNA:

I like to hear it spin.

like to hear it clat - ter as it picks up _____ speed a - gain, re -

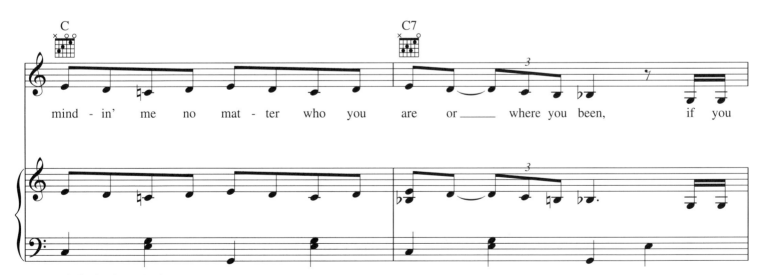

mind - in' me no mat - ter who you are or _____ where you been, if you

Recorded a half step higher.

BRANDED A TRAMP

Music by MARTIN SILVESTRI and JOEL HIGGINS
Lyrics by JOEL HIGGINS

Steady Rock 'n' Roll

Brand - ed a tramp!__ She might as well de - cide__ an - y man who says he

wants her by __ his side _____ will be blush-ing in - stead of the

bride when he mar - ries the tramp.

Slight Calypso feel

Just one __ slip, it does-n't mat - ter who it hap-pens with, __

OLD SANTA FE

Music by MARTIN SILVESTRI and JOEL HIGGINS
Lyrics by JOEL HIGGINS

Mexicali feel

JOHNNY:

rid - er ___ came back on a blis - ter - ing day ___ in the
come from ___ the south bare - ly two years a - go ___ to

Recorded a half step higher.

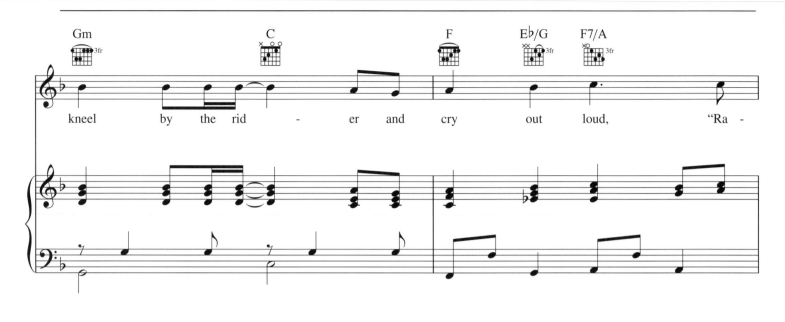

kneel by the rid - er and cry out loud, "Ra-

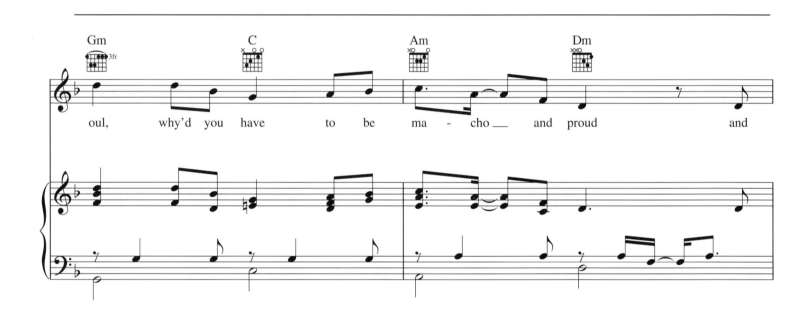

oul, why'd you have to be ma - cho ___ and proud and

take up on Cha - vez - 's dare? He'd

WHAT'S IN IT FOR ME?

Music by MARTIN SILVESTRI and JOEL HIGGINS
Lyrics by JOEL HIGGINS

Calypso-Rock

DANCIN' KID:

What's in it for me? If I ___ were to

stay here and change ___ in the way that you say that you want me to, ___

WHO DO THEY THINK THEY ARE?

Music by MARTIN SILVESTRI and JOEL HIGGINS
Lyrics by JOEL HIGGINS

*Recorded a half step lower.

50

WELCOME HOME

Music by MARTIN SILVESTRI and JOEL HIGGINS
Lyrics by JOEL HIGGINS

Simple Ballad, not too slow

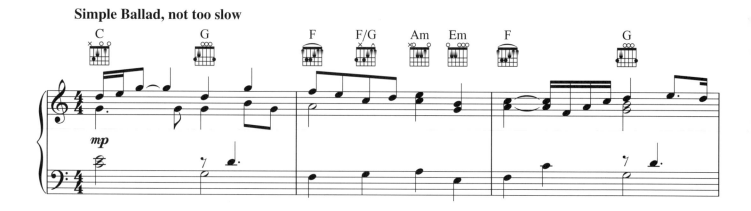

Are you wea-ry? Have you trav-eled much too far? Are you

lone - ly from too long out on ___ the road? Well, be - lieve me, ___ I've been as

bro - ken as you are, so I'm say - in', "Come on in, friend, wel-come home." Wel - come

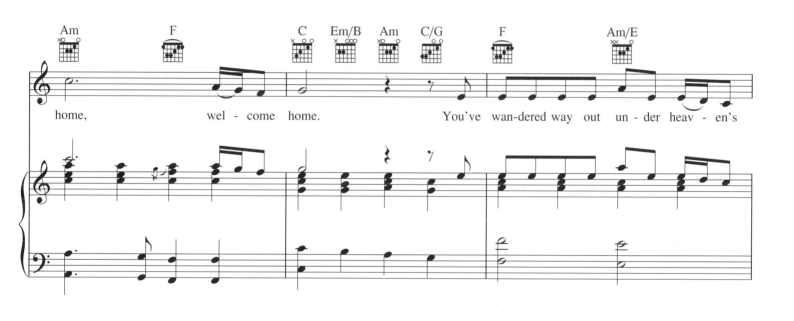

home, wel - come home. You've wan-dered way out un - der heav - en's

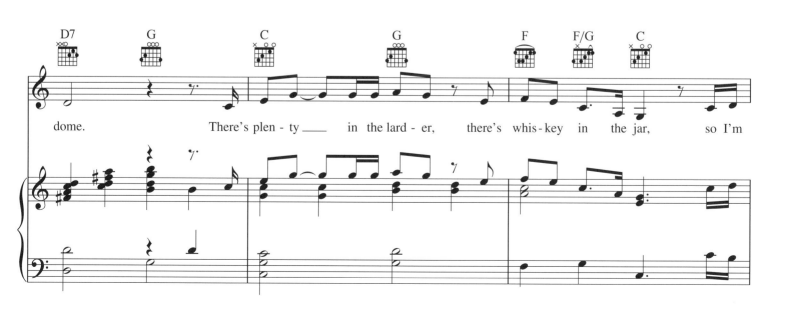

dome. There's plen - ty ____ in the lard - er, there's whis-key in the jar, so I'm

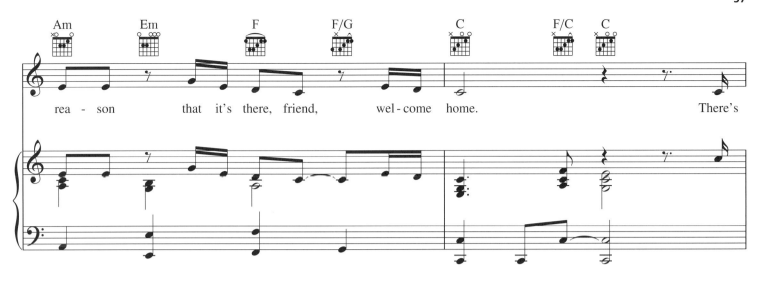

rea - son that it's there, friend, wel - come home. There's

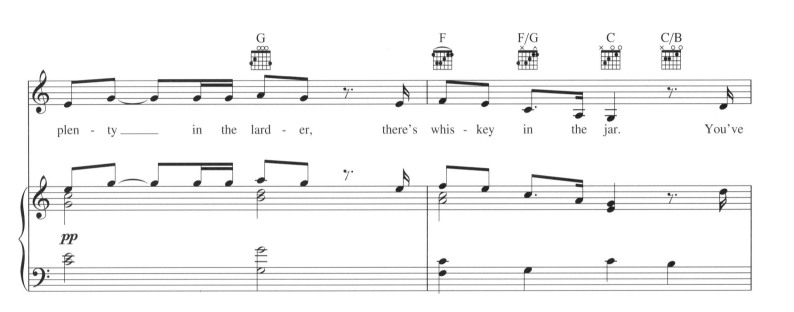

plen - ty ____ in the lard - er, there's whis - key in the jar. You've

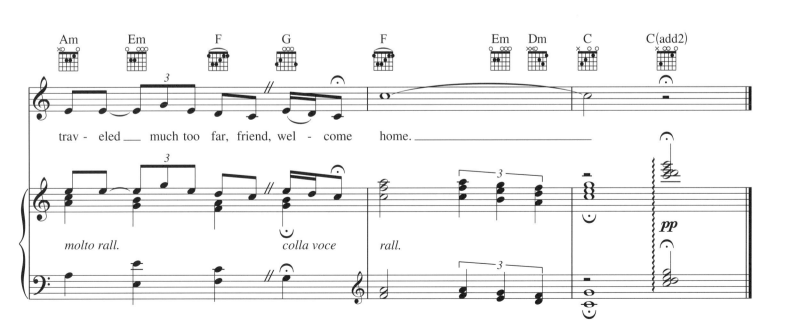

trav - eled ___ much too far, friend, wel - come home. ____

TELL ME A LIE

Music by MARTIN SILVESTRI and JOEL HIGGINS
Lyrics by JOEL HIGGINS

*Recorded a half step higher.

THE GUNFIGHTER

Music by MARTIN SILVESTRI and JOEL HIGGINS
Lyrics by JOEL HIGGINS

Driving finger-style guitar sound

DANCIN' KID:

Look at him, Vienna.

He can't wait to shoot me,   *fingers just*

itchin' to be on a trigger.   *You finally got someone to*

*Recorded a half step lower.

WE'VE HAD OUR MOMENTS

Music by MARTIN SILVESTRI and JOEL HIGGINS
Lyrics by JOEL HIGGINS

*Recorded a half step lower.